Fred Bock Piano Favorites for Majestic Praise

CONTENTS

Lord, I Lift Your Name on High 3
This is the Day 6
I Sing the Greatness of Our God 9
He Has Made Me Glad 12
Blessed Assurance 16
Our God Reigns 18
Halle, Halle, Halle 21
Holy, Holy, Holy 24
A Mighty Fortress is Our God 26
Praise to the Lord, the Almighty 30

Fred Bock Music Company

Lord, I Lift Your Name on High

Rick Founds
Arranged by Fred Bock

Moderato, with rhythmic drive

f
mf
f
ff

f
broaden
ff
8va
5
2
1
1
2
5

This Is the Day

Les Garrett
Arranged by Fred Bock

mf
(echo)
mp
simile
mf
(echo)
mp
mf
mf
like a fanfare
f
mf legato

(echo)
mp
mf
(echo)
mp
mf
scherzo-like
no pedal!
f
l.h.
legato
mf
legato
f
OK to pedal now!
mf
f
8va
ff
l.h.
(ff)
r.h.

I Sing the Greatness of Our God

Fred Bock
Arranged by Fred Bock

slowing
a tempo
r.h.

ten.
rit.
ff
ten.
f
ten.
a tempo
ff
r.h.
8va
8ba

He Has Made Me Glad

Leona Von Brethorst
Arranged by Fred Bock

f
8va

8va
8va
f
8va
ff
no ritard!
mf
both hands 8va
ff
mf

Blessed Assurance

Mrs. J. F. Knapp
Arranged by Fred Bock

a tempo
rit.
ten. ten.
rit.

Our God Reigns

Leonard E. Smith, Jr.
Arranged by Fred Bock

mf
f
r.h.
f

ff
ad lib.
l.h.
ff

Halle, Halle, Halle

Traditional Caribbean
Arranged by Fred Bock

With strength and majesty (♩ =100)

* "Hallelujah Chorus"

Bright and happy

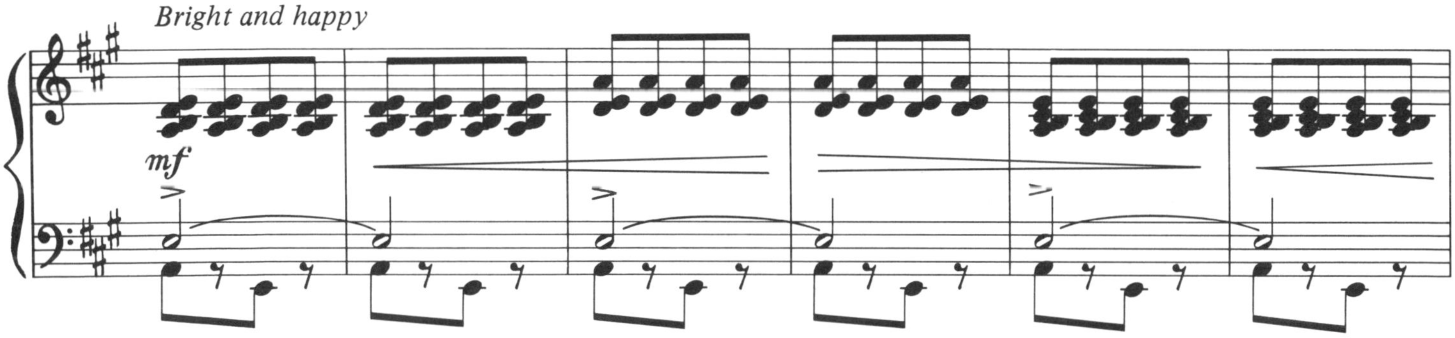

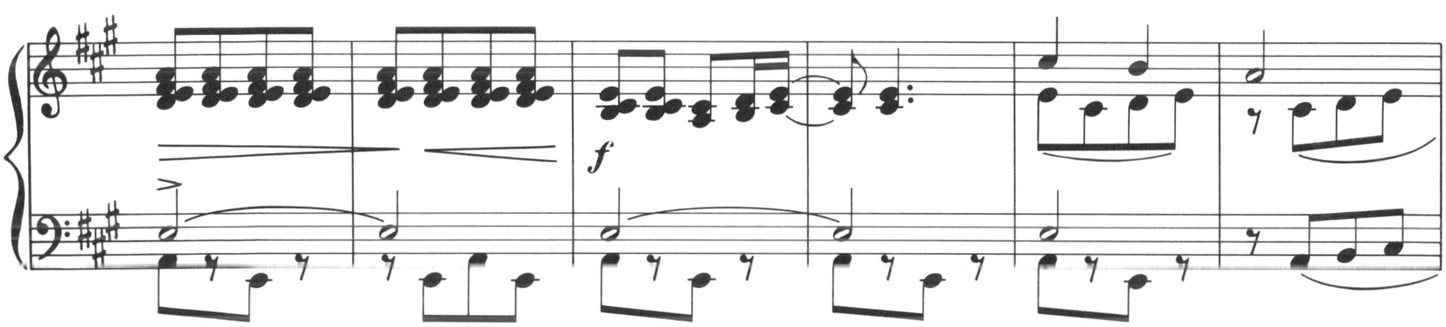

brightly
legato
mf
f
legato
brightly
f
r.h. legato
subito
p

accellerando
Broaden
ff
rit.
brightly
(both hands)
8va
r.h.
l.h.
ff

Holy, Holy, Holy

John B. Dykes
Arranged by Fred Bock

Majestically, with strength

Stately
f
f
ff
8ba

A Mighty Fortress Is Our God

Attributed to Martin Luther
Arranged by Fred Bock

Majestically, but not too slowly

8va
(both hands)
R. H.
L. H.
faster
R. H.
loco
mp
mf

8va (both hands)
f
L. H.
(8va)
loco
f
L. H.
R. H.
8va (both hands)
L. H.
ff
Broaden
8va
ff
8ba
8va
8ba
R. H.
L. H.
8ba
8va
8ba
8va
loco
R. H.
L. H.
8ba

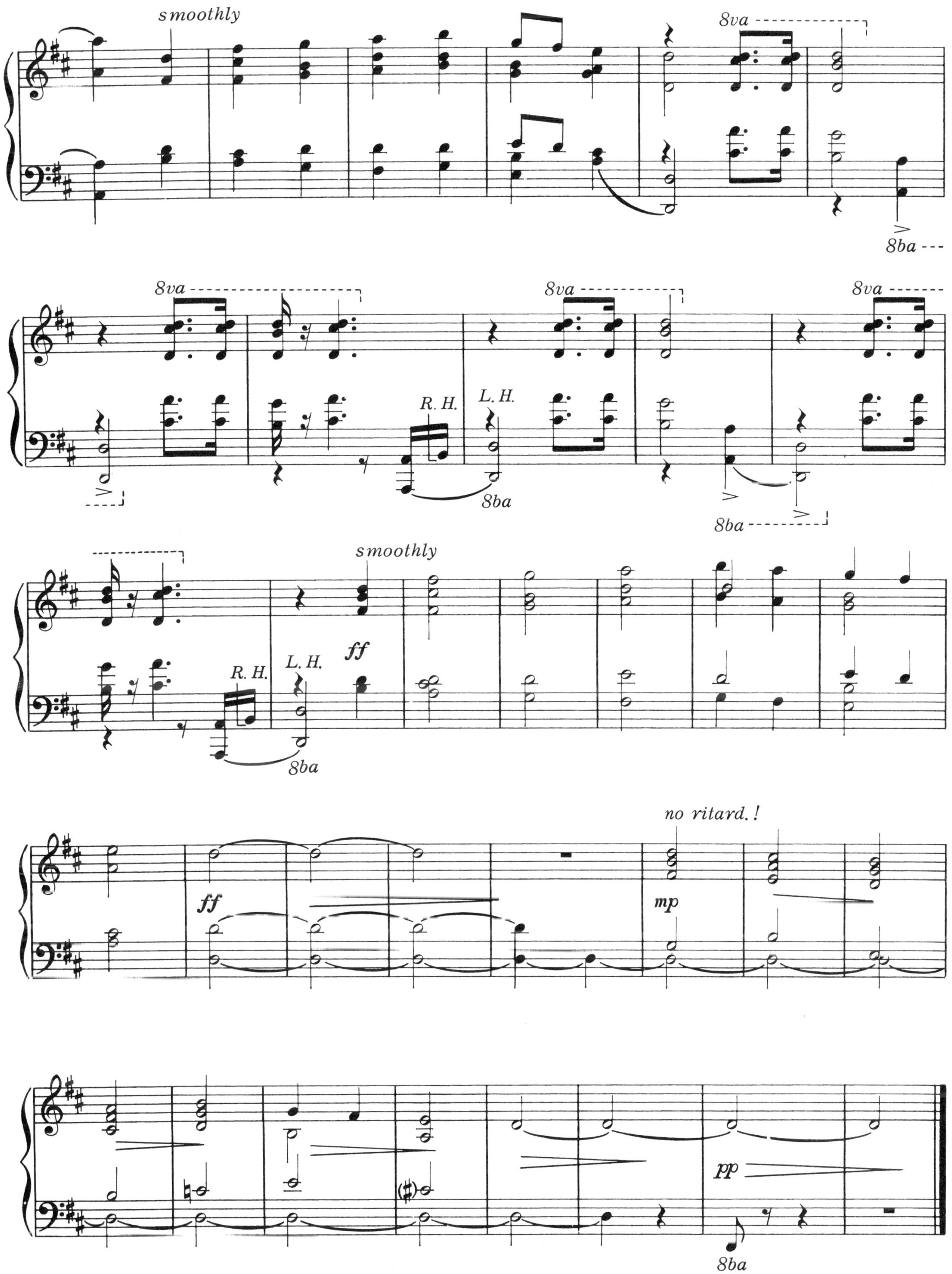
smoothly
8va
8ba
8va
8va
8va
R. H.
L. H.
8ba
8ba
smoothly
R. H.
L. H.
ff
8ba
no ritard.!
ff
mp
pp
8ba

Praise to the Lord, the Almighty

LOBE DEN HERREN
Arranged by Fred Bock

legato

rit.
p
mp
mf
f
ff
Full and strong
f
Stately
mf
lightly
mf
mp
ff
ff
Ped.